Easter
ACTIVITY BOOK

THIS BOOK IS ALL YOURS. BEFORE YOU START YOUR FUN EASTER ADVENTURE, WRITE YOUR NAME AND A SPECIAL MESSAGE OR WISH.
LET'S MAKE THIS BOOK TRULY YOURS!

My Name:

_____

My Special Message

_____
_____
_____
_____

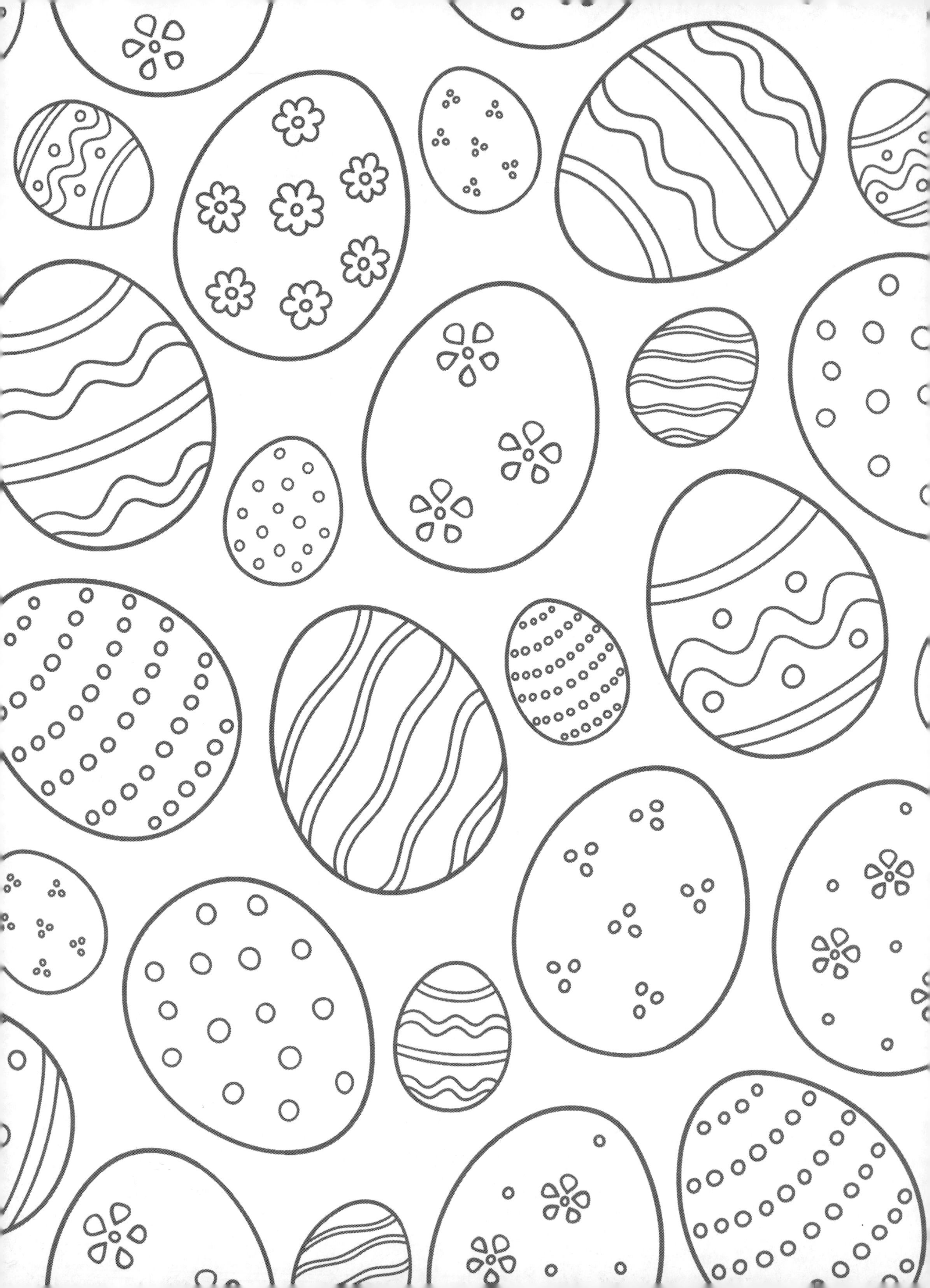

HELLO LITTLE BUNNY!

I'M SO HAPPY YOU'RE HERE TO HOP INTO A WORLD OF EASTER FUN! JUMP, GIGGLE, AND LET YOUR SMILE SHINE BRIGHT.

REMEMBER, EVERY BUNNY IS SPECIAL—ESPECIALLY YOU.

HAPPY EASTER AND LET THE FUN BEGIN!

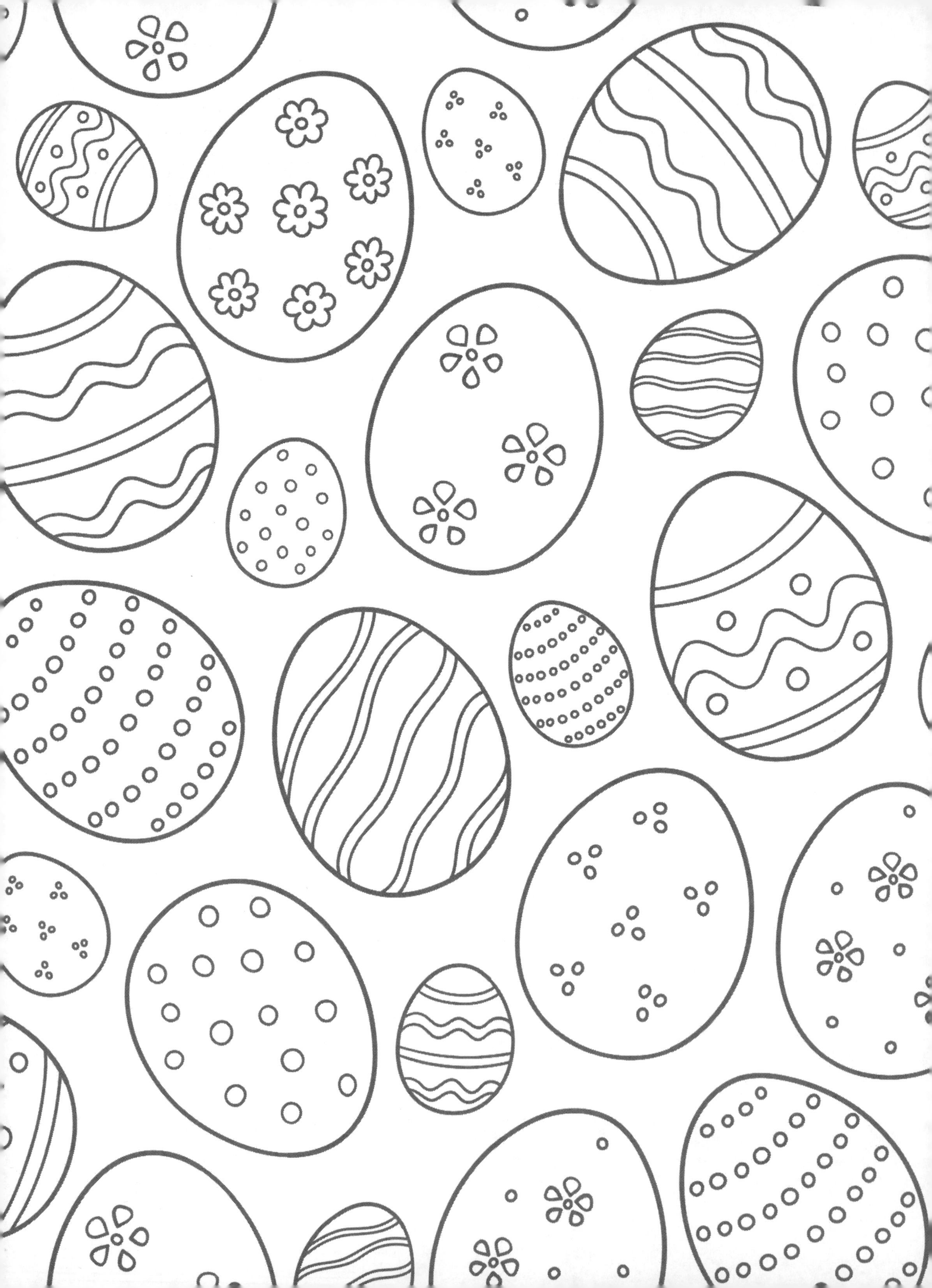

EASTER EGG LINE TRACING

TRACE THE DOTS TO MATCH THE EGG ON THE LEFT TO ITS BASKET ON THE RIGHT.

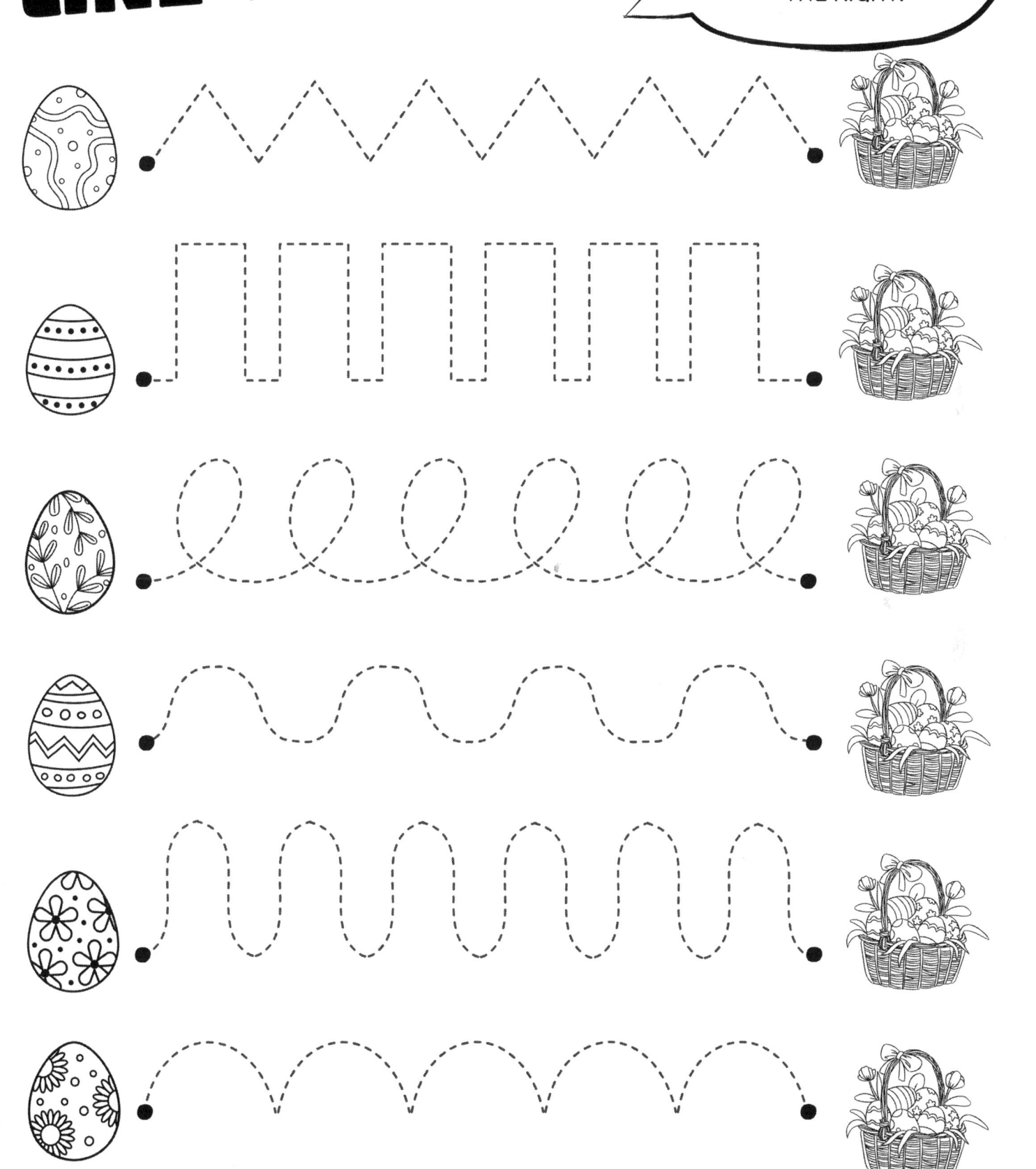

HELP EACH EASTER FRIEND FIND THEIR SPECIAL TREAT!

FIND THE WAY OUT AND MATCH EACH CHARACTER TO THE RIGHT GIFT.

EASTER EGG TRACING

TRACE THE DOTTED LINES ON EACH EGG AND THEN COLOR THEM HOWEVER YOU LIKE

1. WHAT DO YOU CALL A BUNNY THAT TELLS SECRETS?

2. WHAT DO YOU CALL AN EGG WHO IS A SUPERHERO?

1. A HUSH-HARE!
2. EGG-MAN!

FIND THE SHAPE TWIN

FIND ONE WITH THE SAME SHAPE AND PAINT IT IN THE APPROPRIATE COLORS

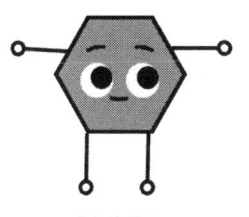

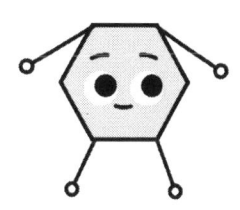

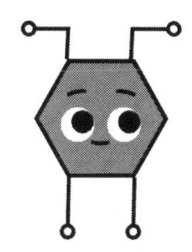

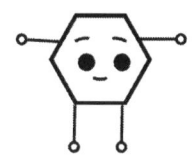

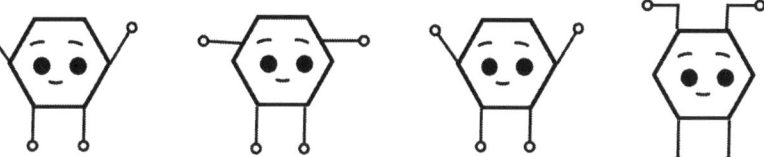

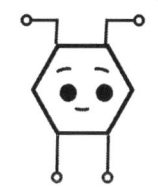

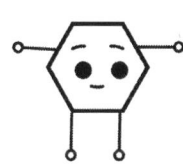

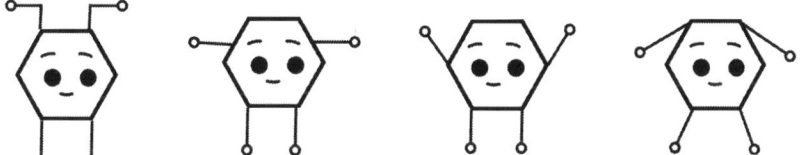

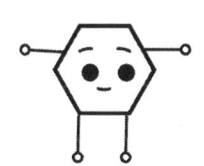

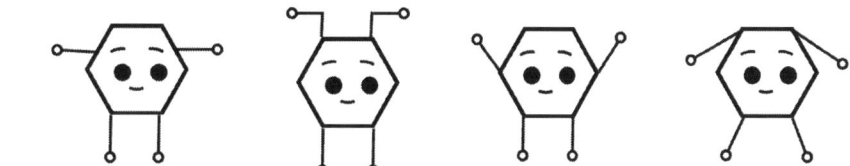

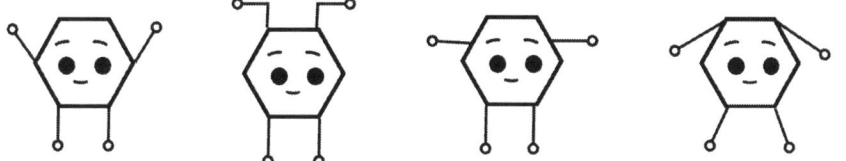

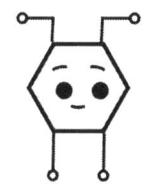

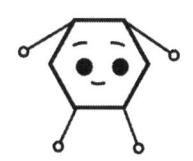

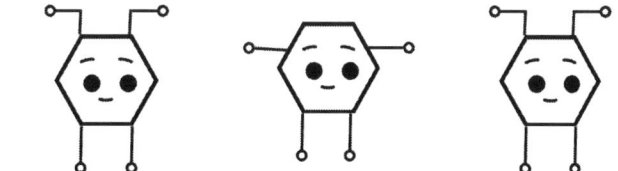

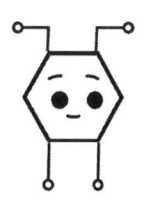

RED **BLUE** **YELLOW** **GREEN**

LEFT OR RIGHT?

DRAW A CIRCLE AROUND ALL THE ANIMALS FACING LEFT AND COLOR ALL THE ANIMALS FACING RIGHT.

ANIMAL TRACING

TRACE THE DOTTED LINES ON EACH FRIENDLY CRITTER, THEN COLOR THEM ANY WAY YOU LIKE. HAVE FUN!

3. HOW DO BUNNIES SEND MESSAGES?

4. HOW DO YOU CATCH A UNIQUE BUNNY?

3. BY HARE-MAIL!
4. UNIQUE UP ON IT!

ANIMAL TRACING

TRACE THE DOTTED LINES ON EACH FRIENDLY CRITTER, THEN COLOR THEM ANY WAY YOU LIKE. HAVE FUN!

FINISH THE PICTURE

DRAW THE OTHER HALVES, COLOR THE PICTURES AND TRACE THE WORDS.

BUNNY

EGG

BASKET

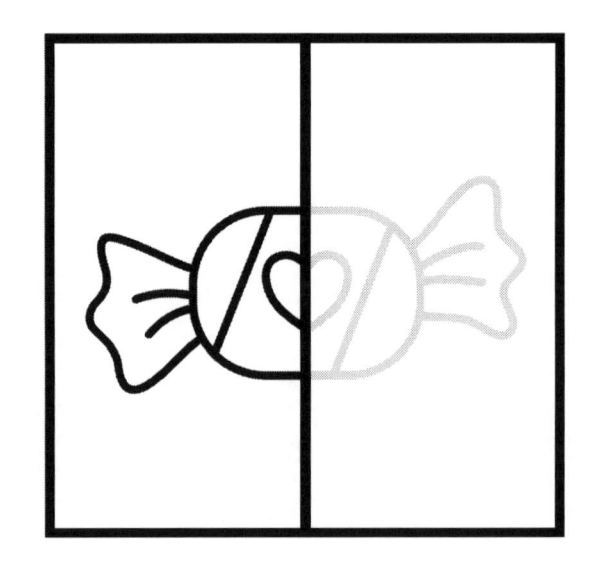

CANDY

COMPLETE THE EGG DESIGN

COPY THE PATTERNS ONTO THE BLANK HALF TO FINISH EACH EASTER EGG. THEN COLOR THEM IN ANY WAY YOU LIKE!

SYMMETRY DRAWING

USE THE GRID TO DRAW THE OTHER SIDE OF EACH IMAGE

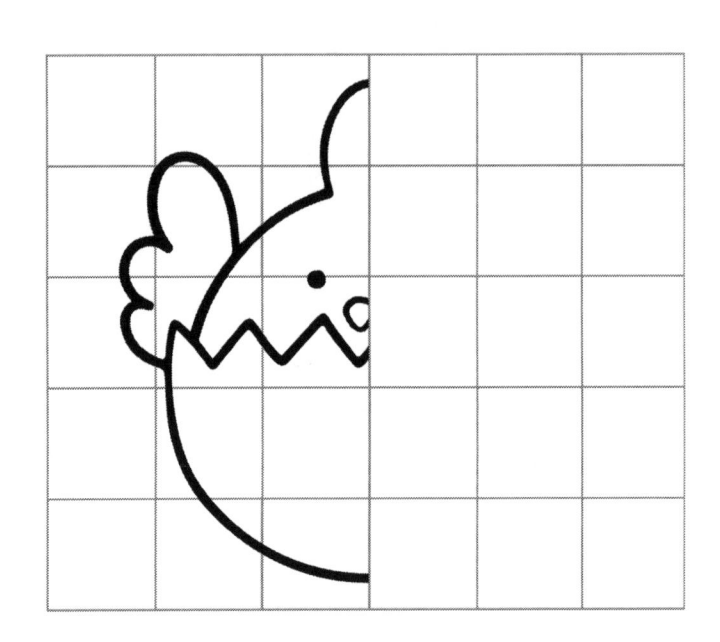

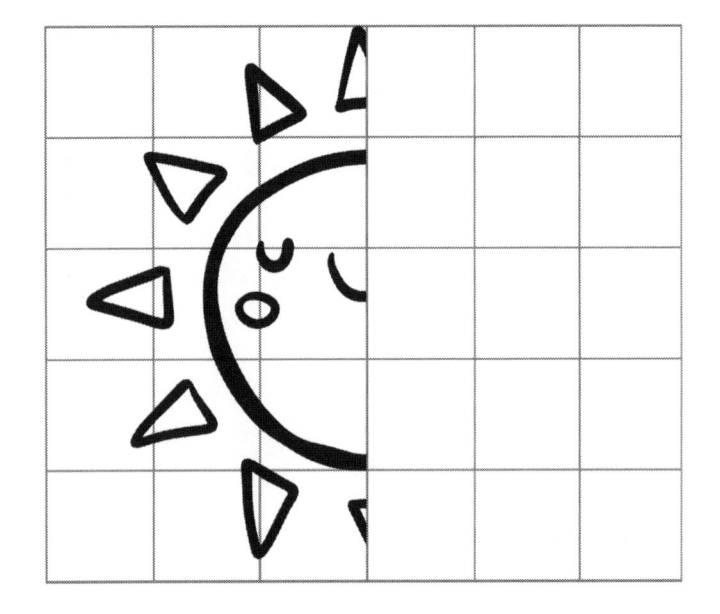

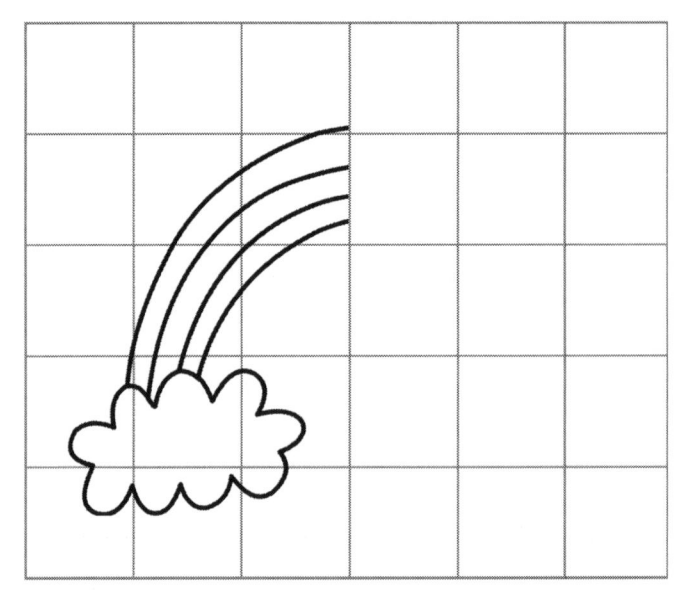

SYMMETRY DRAWING

USE THE GRID TO DRAW THE OTHER SIDE OF EACH IMAGE

MAZE CHALLENGE

HELP THE BOY FIND HIS WAY THROUGH THE MAZE TO COLLECT THE EASTER EGGS IN THE CENTER. GOOD LUCK!

START

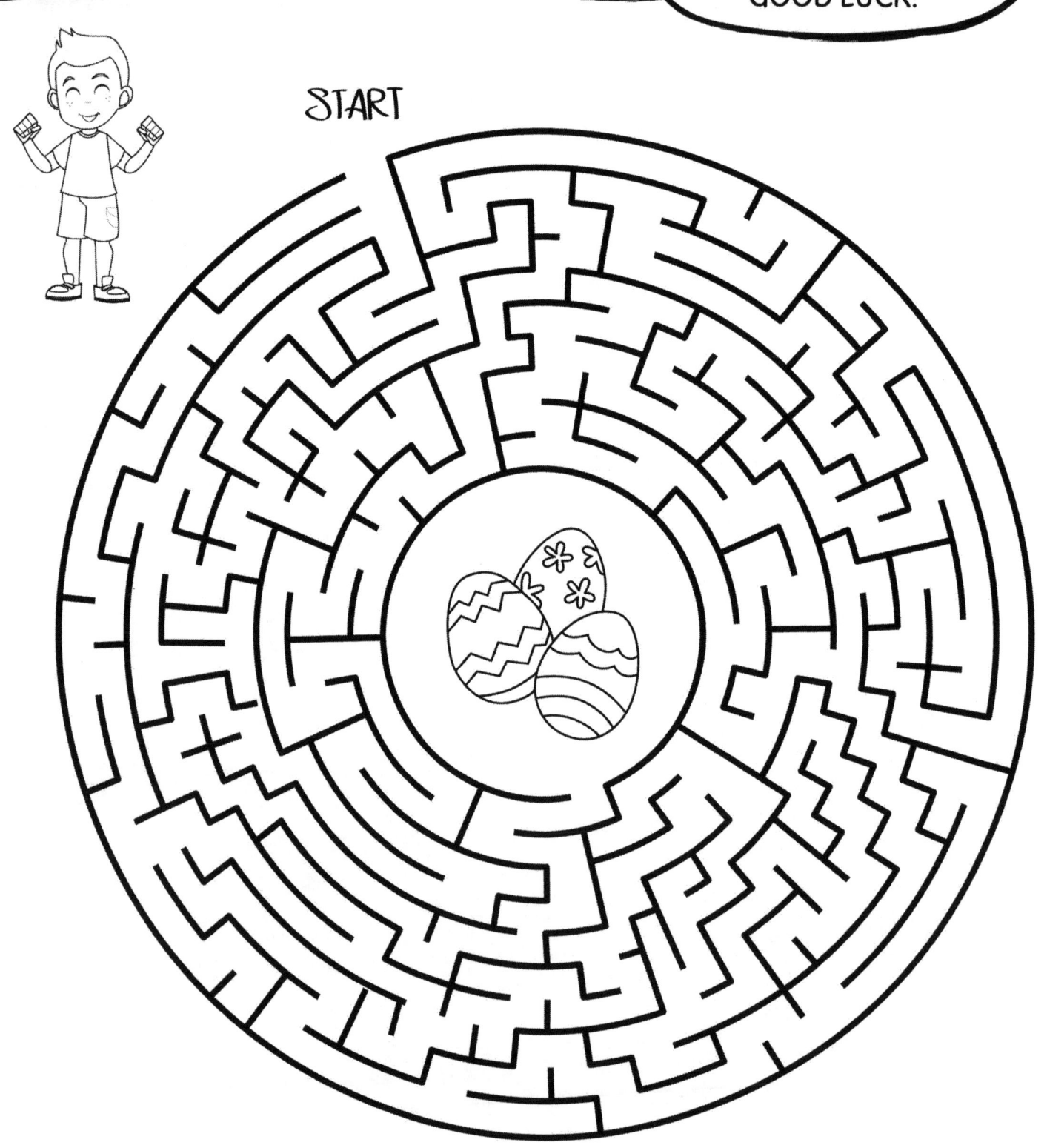

MAZE CHALLENGE

TRACE THE PATH THROUGH THE MAZE TO BRING THEM TOGETHER. GOOD LUCK!

Happy Easter!

START

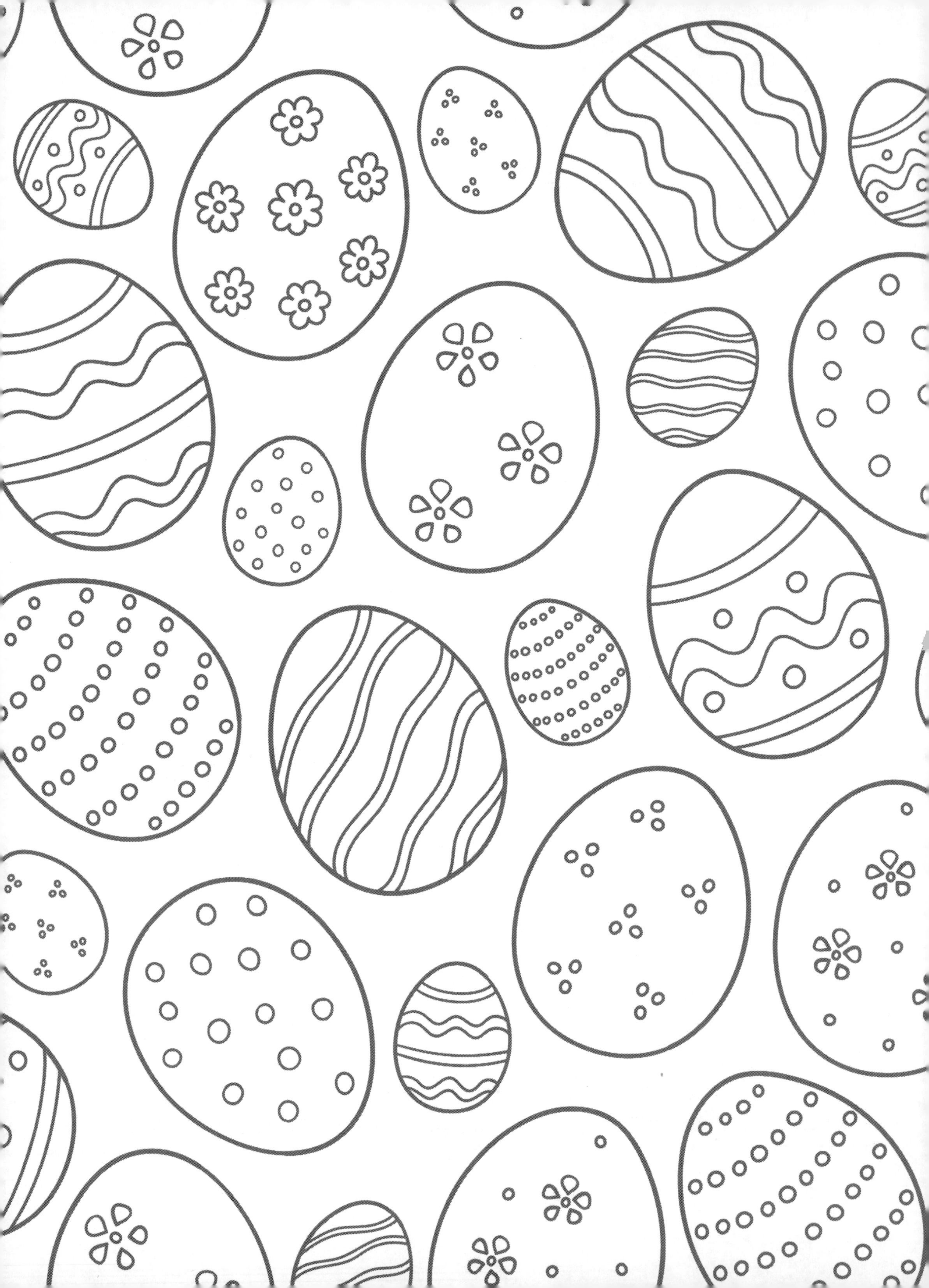

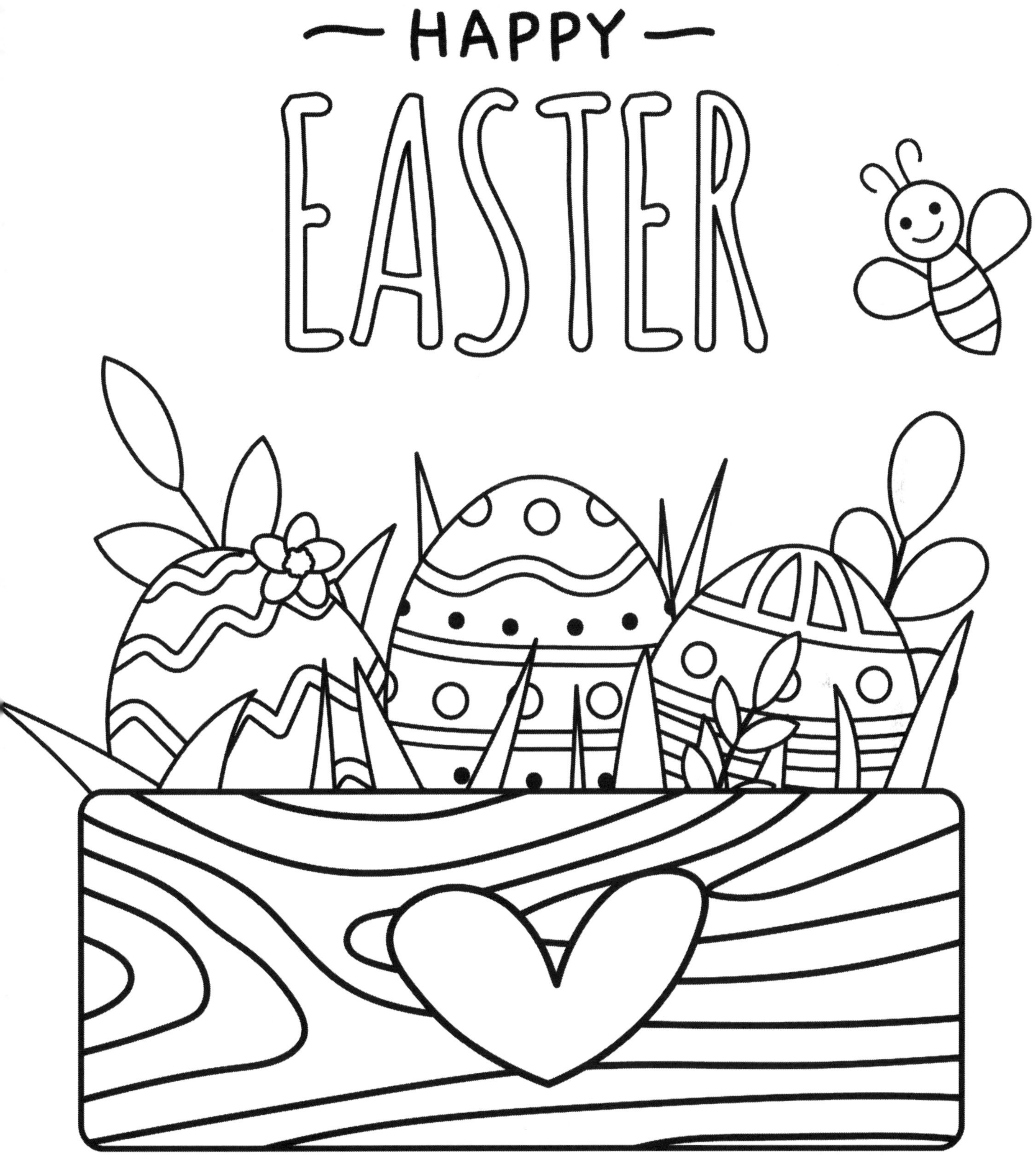
HAPPY
EASTER

WHY DID THE EASTER EGG HIDE?

BECAUSE IT WAS A LITTLE CHICKEN!

WHY DOES THE EASTER BUNNY LOVE TO DANCE?

BECAUSE HE'S GOT THE BEST HOP AROUND!

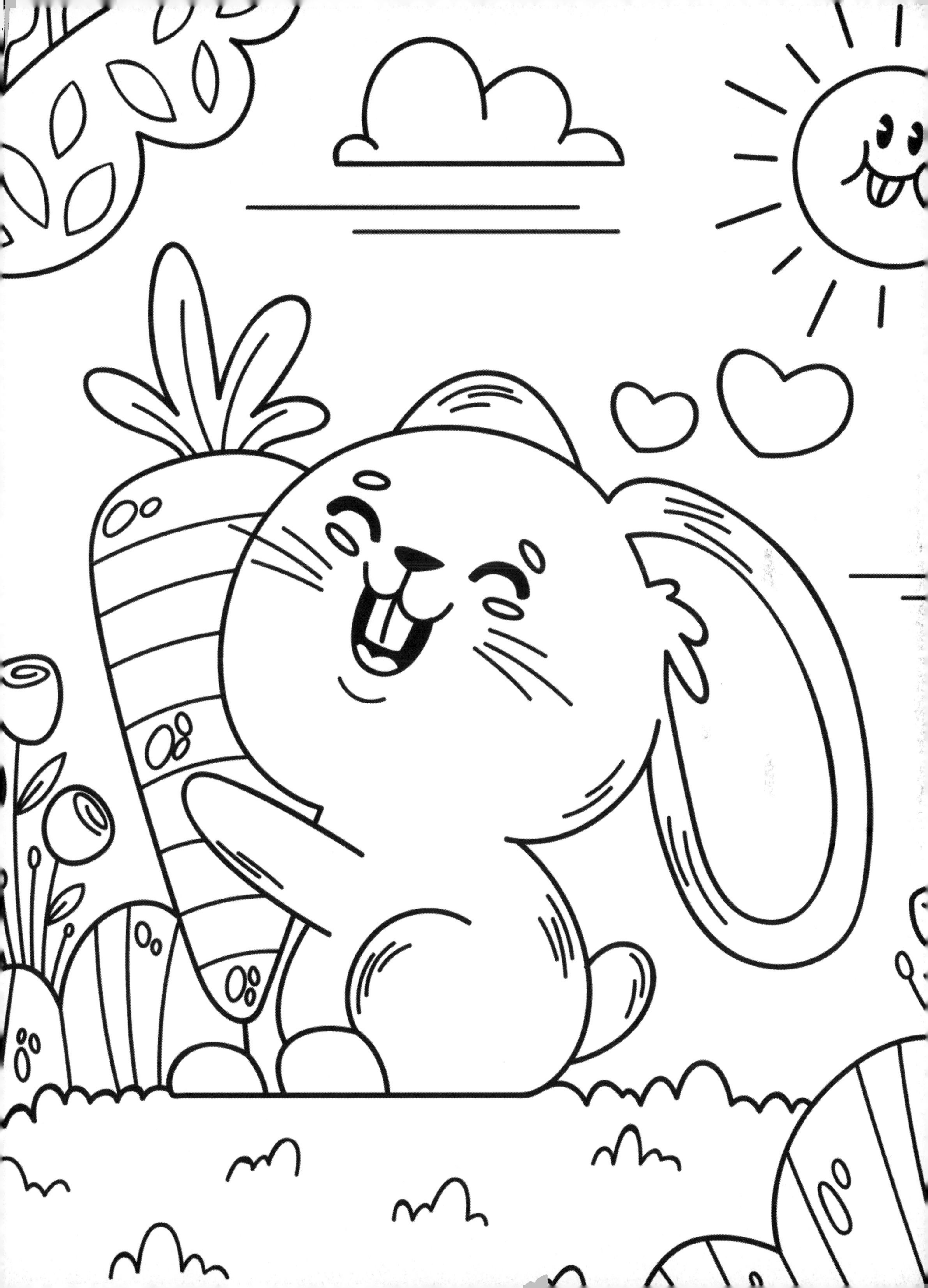

HOW DOES THE EASTER BUNNY STAY HEALTHY?

HE DOES LOTS OF EGG-CERCISE!

WHERE DO SICK BUNNIES GO?

TO THE HOP-SPITAL!

TRACE AND WRITE

> TRACE THE DOTTED LETTERS TO PRACTICE WRITING THESE FUN WORDS. FOLLOW ALONG CAREFULLY, THEN TRY WRITING THE WORD ON YOUR OWN!

EASTER

E

BUNNY

B

EGG

E

TRACE AND WRITE

TRACE THE DOTTED LETTERS TO PRACTICE WRITING THESE FUN WORDS. FOLLOW ALONG CAREFULLY, THEN TRY WRITING THE WORD ON YOUR OWN!

BASKET

B

CHICK

C

CARROT

C

TRACE AND WRITE

> TRACE THE DOTTED LETTERS TO PRACTICE WRITING THESE FUN WORDS. FOLLOW ALONG CAREFULLY, THEN TRY WRITING THE WORD ON YOUR OWN!

TULIP

T

SPRING

S

CANDY

C

COMPLETE THE WORD

> FILL IN THE MISSING LETTERS TO COMPLETE EACH WORD. LOOK AT THE CLUES AND THINK ABOUT THE WORD YOU KNOW FROM EASTER TIME!

I

| C | H | | C | |

K

U

| B | | N | N | |

Y

COMPLETE THE WORD

FILL IN THE MISSING LETTERS TO COMPLETE EACH WORD. LOOK AT THE CLUES AND THINK ABOUT THE WORD YOU KNOW FROM EASTER TIME!

| L | | M | B |

A

| E | | G |

G

5. WHAT DID THE EGG SAY TO THE CLOWN?

6. WHY DID THE BUNNY BRING A PEN TO SCHOOL?

5. YOU CRACK ME UP!
6. BECAUSE HE WANTED TO DRAW ATTENTION!

COMPLETE THE WORD

FILL IN THE MISSING LETTERS TO COMPLETE EACH WORD. LOOK AT THE CLUES AND THINK ABOUT THE WORD YOU KNOW FROM EASTER TIME!

G

| S | P | R | | R | | N | |

I

| B | | S | K | | T |

A

E

READ AND COLOR

READ COLOR WORD AND COLOR THE EASTER ITEMS.

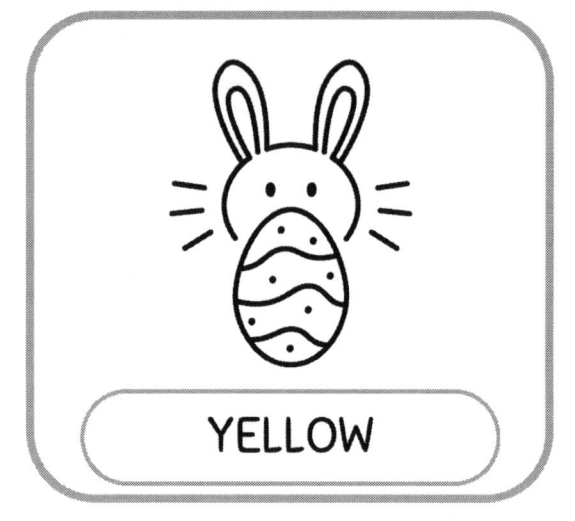

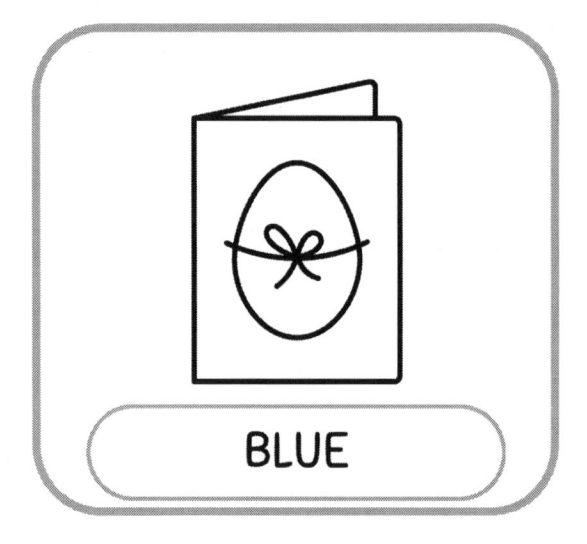

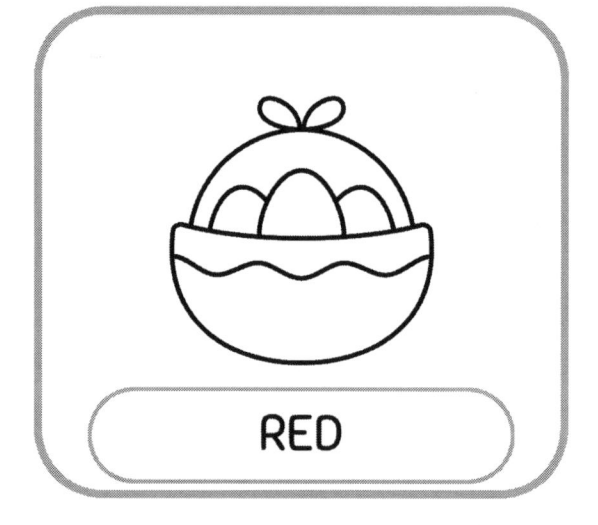

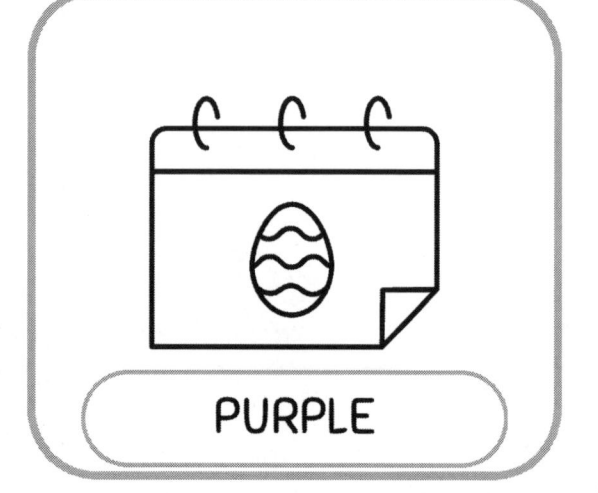

YELLOW	GREEN
BLUE	RED
PINK	PURPLE

7. WHAT DO YOU CALL A BUNNY WHO FIXES THINGS?

8. WHAT DO YOU GET WHEN YOU CROSS A BUNNY WITH A SPIDER?

7. A HANDY HARE!
8. A HARE-NET!

WORD SEARCH

> FIND AND CIRCLE EACH HIDDEN WORD. THEY APPEAR HORIZONTALLY OR VERTICALLY. GOOD LUCK

```
T O E G G B R P B H D C
R X E F I R I T U K E H
A A R L D B N T N A N O
D E C O R A T E N S T C
I A E W I S E R Y U A O
T O I E N K N N O L L L
I O R R A E I C C N A A
O A E S A T U C K Y M T
N O S E S P R I N G B E
N P A T T E R N C H K O
S F L O S S L O V E A L
E A S T E R H O E N E D
```

- ~~EGG~~
- LAMB
- SUNNY
- PATTERN
- BASKET
- SPRING
- TRADITION
- DECORATE
- CHOCOLATE
- BUNNY
- EASTER
- FLOWERS

EMOTION CROSSWORD

LOOK AT EACH NUMBERED FACE AND GUESS THE CORRESPONDING EMOTION. WRITE THE WORD IN THE CROSSWORD FOLLOWING THE NUMBERS.

5 ↓ C N C N N D

4 → _ N L V _

1 → S _

3 ↓ G R

3 → H _ P _

FOUR SEASONS CROSSWORD

LOOK AT EACH PICTURE OF THE TREE AND DECIDE WHICH SEASON IT SHOWS. LABEL THE IMAGES AND COLOR THE SCENES AS YOU LIKE.

1.

2.

3.

4.

FOUR SEASONS CROSSWORD

FILL IN THE CROSSWORD WITH THE FOUR SEASON NAMES

4.

2. → S _ M M _ _

T _ M

3. W _ N T _ _

P

I

WORD SEARCH

FIND AND CIRCLE EACH HIDDEN WORD. THEY APPEAR HORIZONTALLY OR VERTICALLY. GOOD LUCK

T	O	S	U	N	B	R	P	B	H	D	C
R	X	M	F	I	R	I	T	I	K	E	L
P	A	I	L	D	B	N	T	R	A	N	O
L	E	L	O	R	A	T	R	D	S	T	U
A	A	E	W	I	S	E	E	Y	U	A	D
Y	O	I	E	N	K	N	E	O	N	L	H
I	O	R	R	A	I	N	C	C	N	A	A
O	A	E	S	A	T	U	C	K	Y	M	K
N	O	S	E	G	R	A	S	S	G	B	E
N	P	H	A	P	P	Y	N	C	H	U	O
S	F	L	O	S	S	L	O	V	E	G	L
S	K	Y	T	U	R	H	O	E	N	E	D

- ~~SUN~~
- RAIN
- SMILE
- SKY
- BIRD
- PLAY
- TREE
- FLOWER
- BUG
- CLOUD
- GRASS
- HAPPY

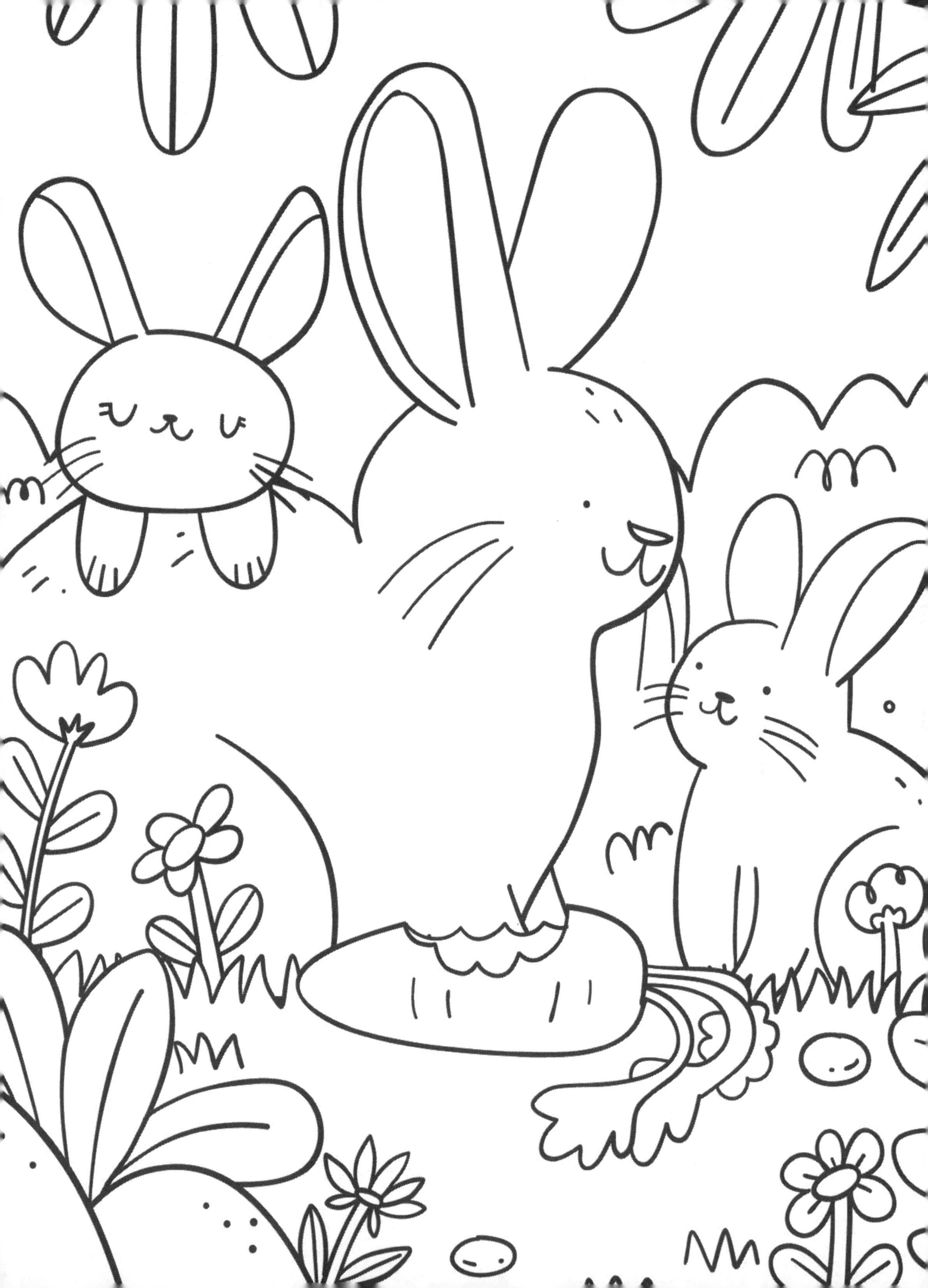

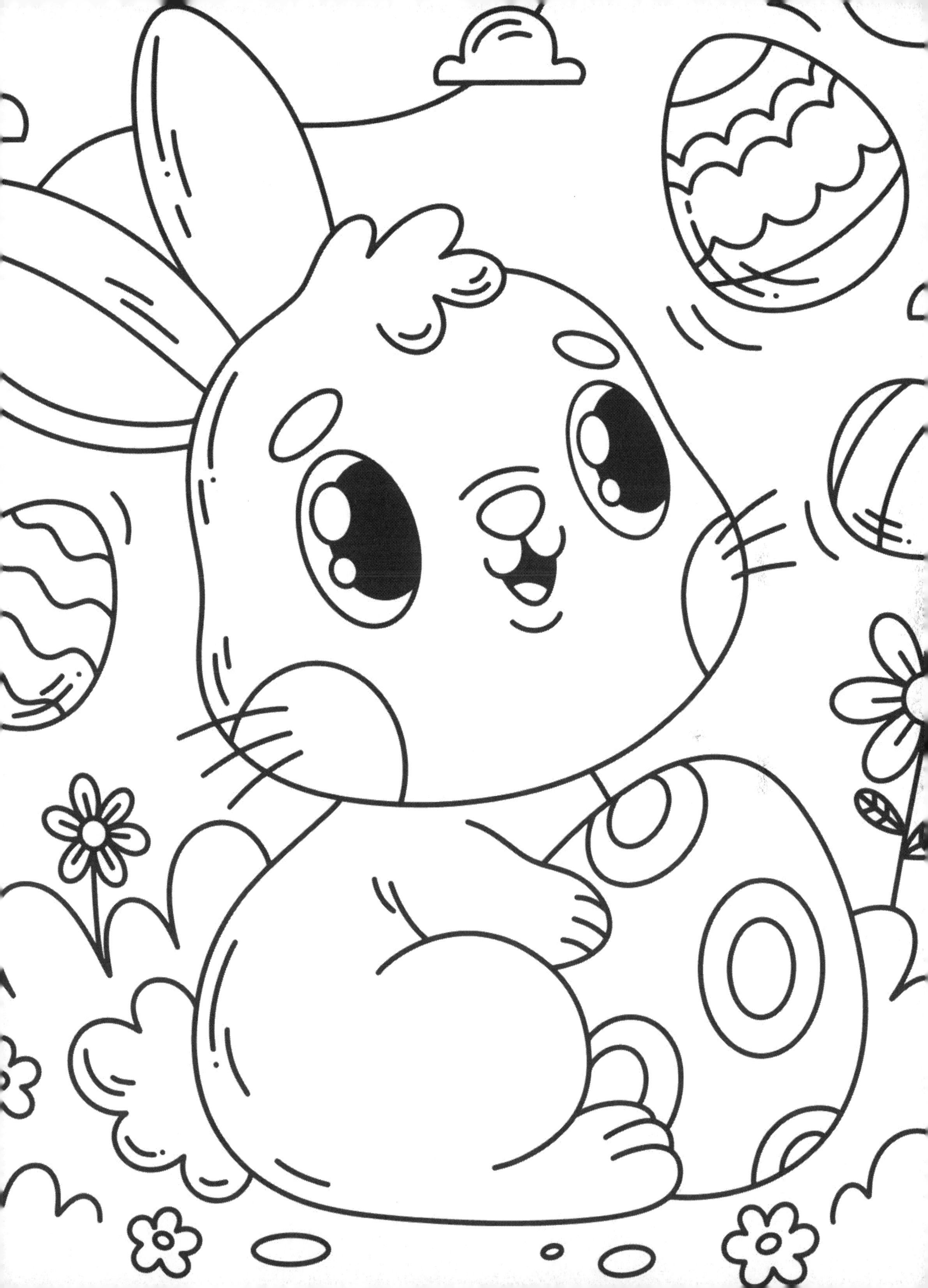

EASTER COUNT

COLOR, COUNT AND WRITE THE NUMBERS IN THE BOXES BELOW

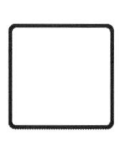

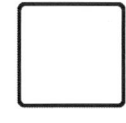

GUESS THE WORD

> READ EACH RIDDLE AND WRITE DOWN THE WORD YOU THINK IS THE ANSWER. USE YOUR EASTER KNOWLEDGE AND HAVE FUN!

1. HOW DOES THE EASTER BUNNY STAY HEALTHY?

2. I COME IN A SHELL, AND YOU MIGHT FIND SURPRISES INSIDE. WHAT AM I?"

1. BUNNY
2. EGG

EASTER COUNT

COLOR, COUNT AND WRITE THE NUMBERS IN THE BOXES BELOW

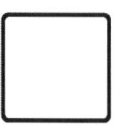

I'M SMALL AND YELLOW, I CHIRP AND PEEP IN THE SPRING. WHO AM I?

I'M LONG AND CRUNCHY, AND RABBITS LOVE TO MUNCH ON ME. WHAT AM I?

3. CHICK
4. CARROT

DOT TO DOT

FOLLOW THE NUMBERS TO CONNECT EACH DOT.

DOT TO DOT

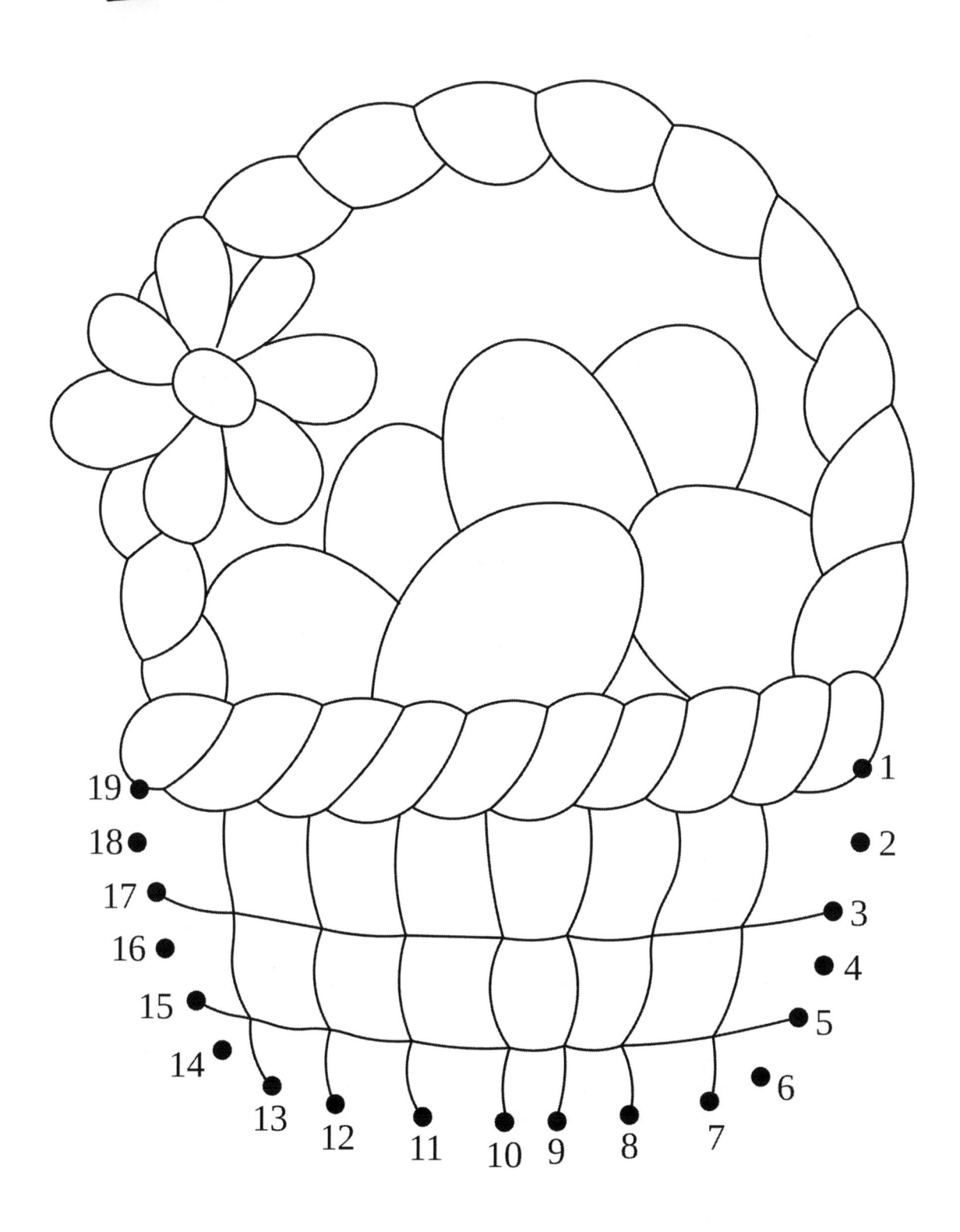

FOLLOW THE NUMBERS TO CONNECT EACH DOT.

DOT TO DOT

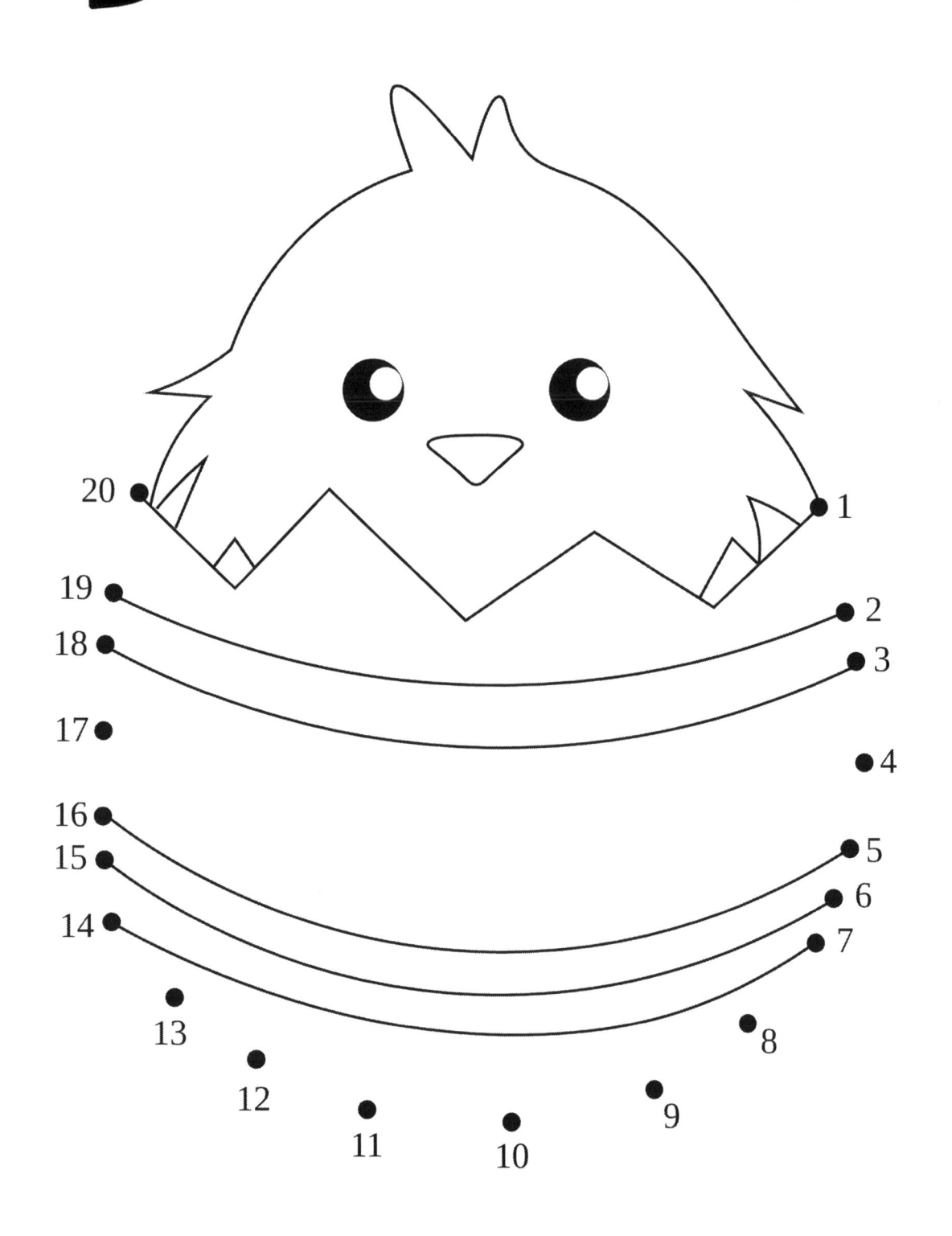

FOLLOW THE NUMBERS TO CONNECT EACH DOT.

DOT TO DOT

FOLLOW THE NUMBERS TO CONNECT EACH DOT.

22 1
    2
21
      3
20
        4

19   5

18   6

17   7

16   8

15   9

14   10
    13   11
       12

DOT TO DOT

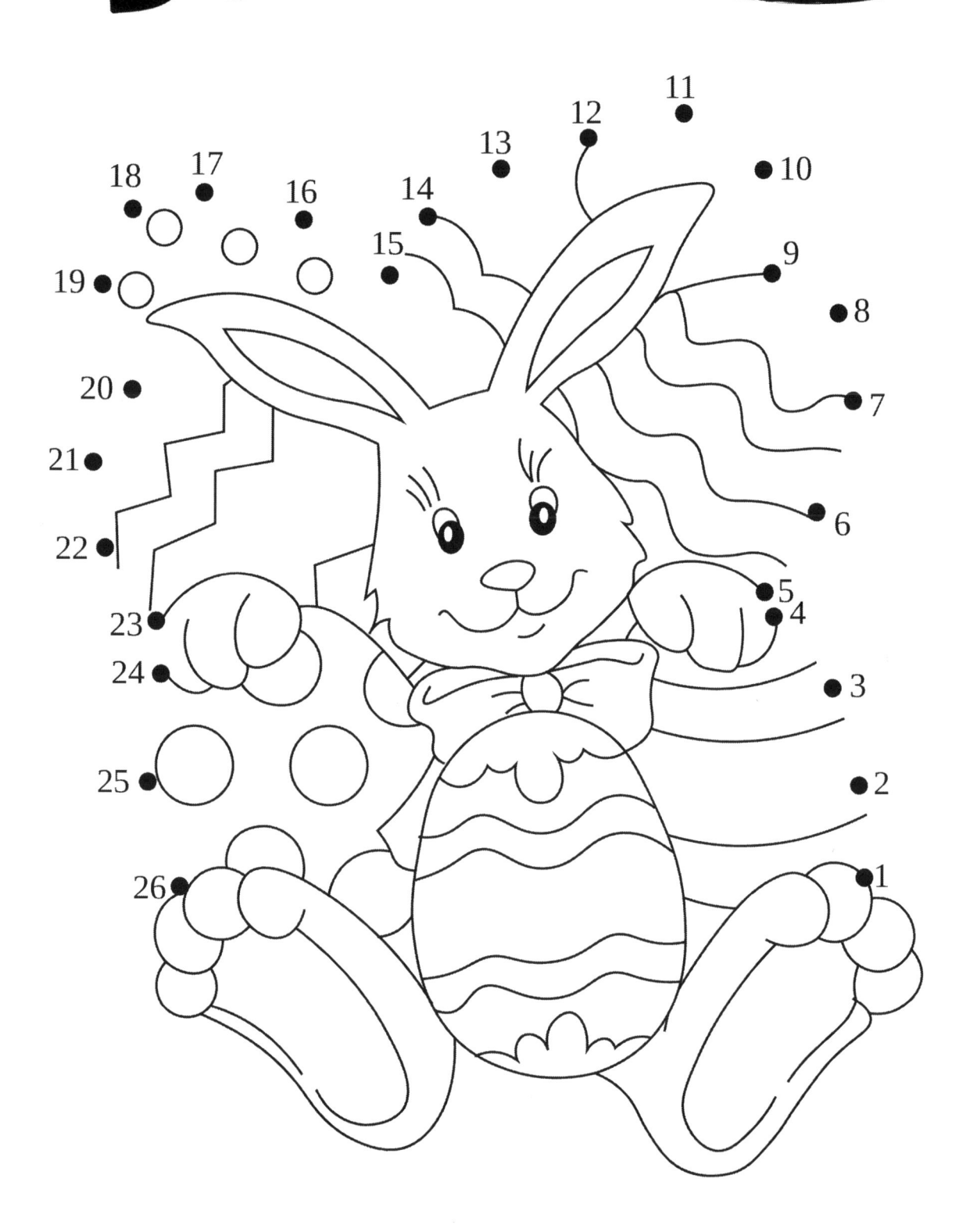

FOLLOW THE NUMBERS TO CONNECT EACH DOT.

COLOR BY NUMBER

USE THE COLOR KEY TO BRING YOUR EASTER UNICORN TO LIFE

7	RED	5	BROWN
4	PINK	2	LIGHT BLUE
3	YELLOW	1	ORANGE

COLOR BY NUMBER

USE THE COLOR KEY TO BRING YOUR EASTER UNICORN TO LIFE

7	RED	5	GREEN
4	PINK	2	LIGHT BLUE
3	YELLOW	1	BLUE

MATH & COLOR FUN!

PLAY WITH ADDITION AND DISCOVER THE RIGHT COLOR

MATH & COLOR FUN!

PLAY WITH ADDITION AND DISCOVER THE RIGHT COLOR

2+4=____ BROWN

3+2=____ ORANGE

6+1=____ SKY BLUE

8+1=____ DARK GREEN

1+1=____ DARK PINK

1+2=____ LIGHT BLUE

2+2=____ YELLOW

4+4=____ LIGHT GREEN

| 1 | PINK

COLOR BY NUMBER

PLAY WITH SUBTRACTION AND FIND THE RIGHT COLOR

MATH & COLOR FUN!

PLAY WITH SUBTRACTION AND FIND THE RIGHT COLOR

4-1= ____ RED

6-1= ____ ORANGE

9-2= ____ SKY BLUE

10-1= ____ DARK GREEN

3-1= ____ DARK PINK

6-2= ____ LIGHT PINK

8-2= ____ YELLOW

10-2= ____ LIGHT GREEN

| 1 | LIGHT BLUE

DOT TO DOT

FOLLOW THE NUMBERS TO CONNECT EACH DOT.

COUNT AND CIRCLE

COUNT THE BUNNIES OR CHICKS, THEN CIRCLE THE CORRECT NUMBER

6
4
7

3
6
5

COUNT AND CIRCLE

COUNT THE EGGS OR BASKETS, THEN CIRCLE THE CORRECT NUMBER

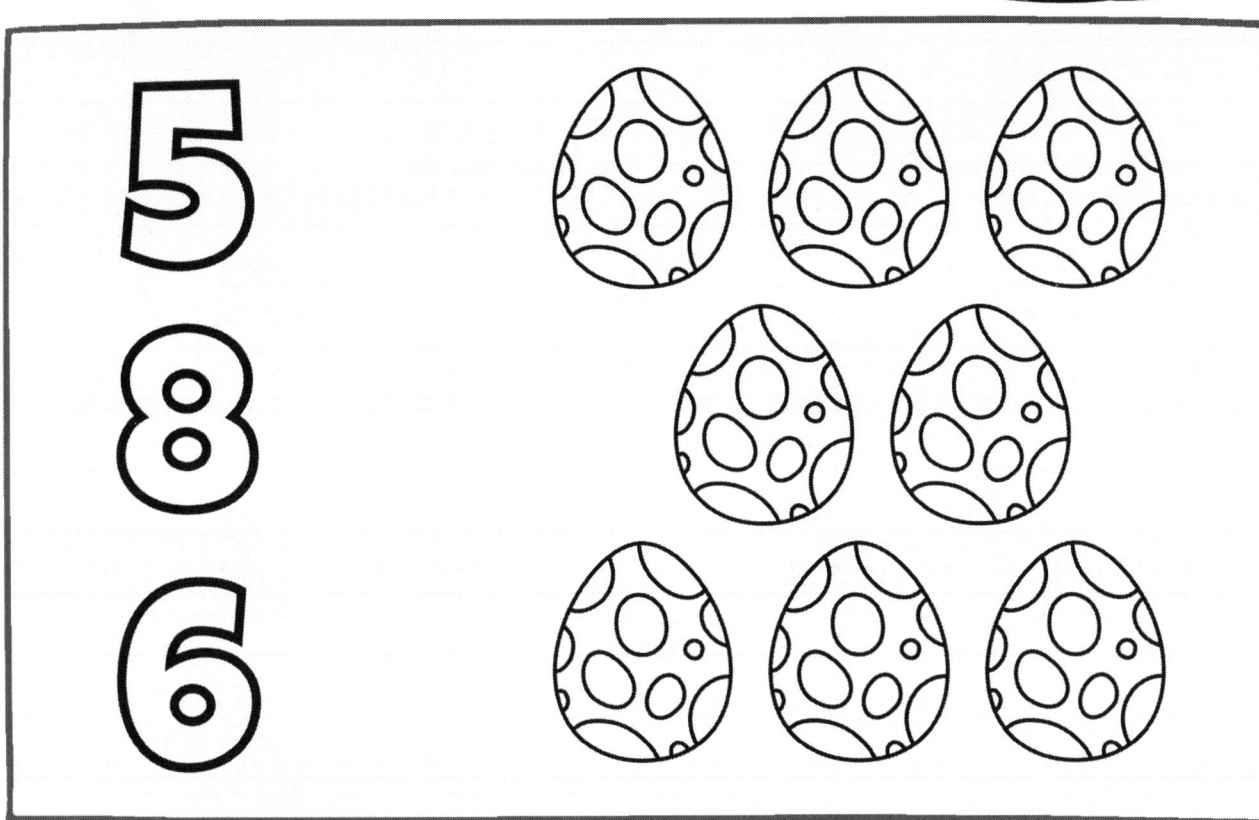

5
8
6

8
5
6

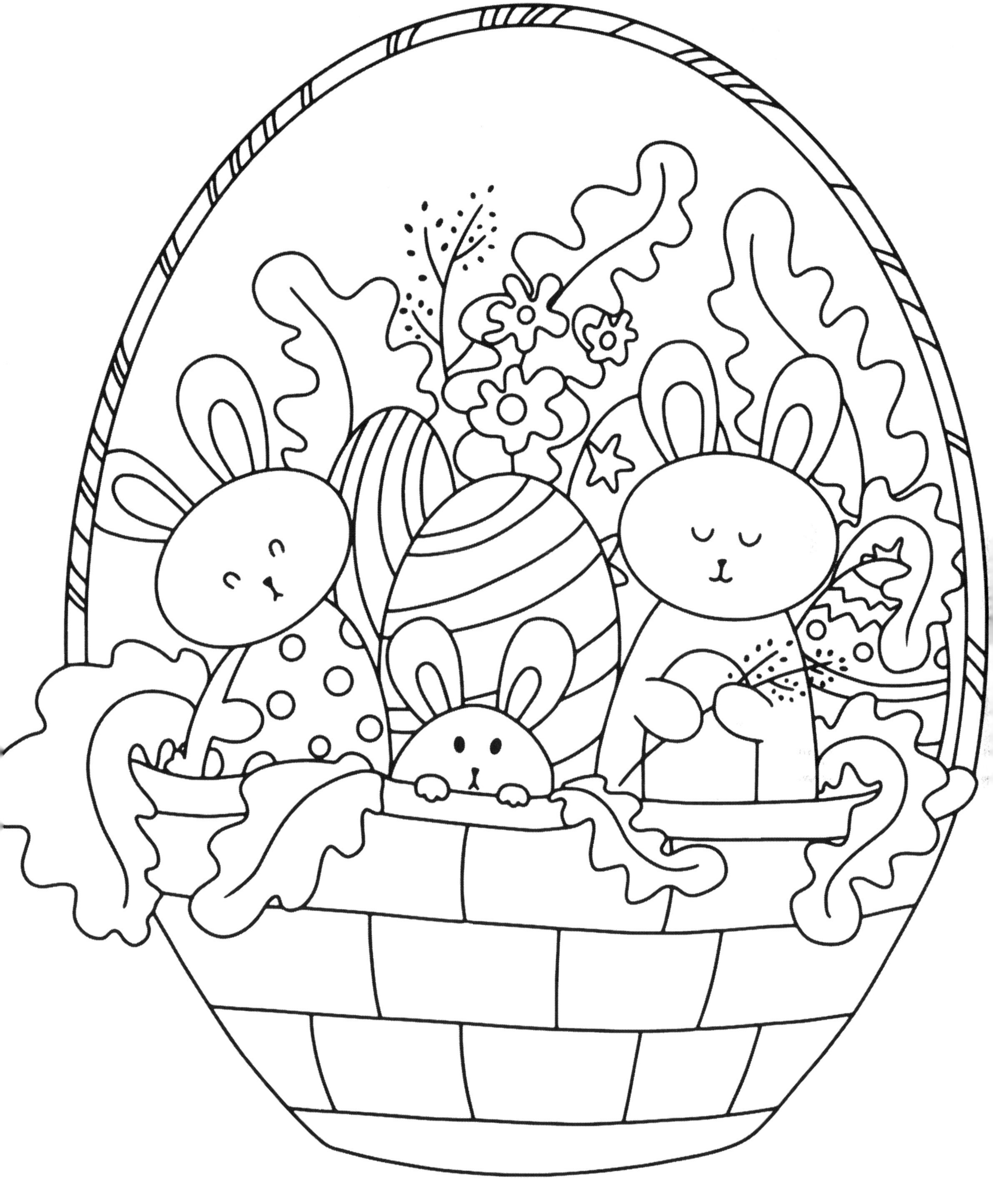

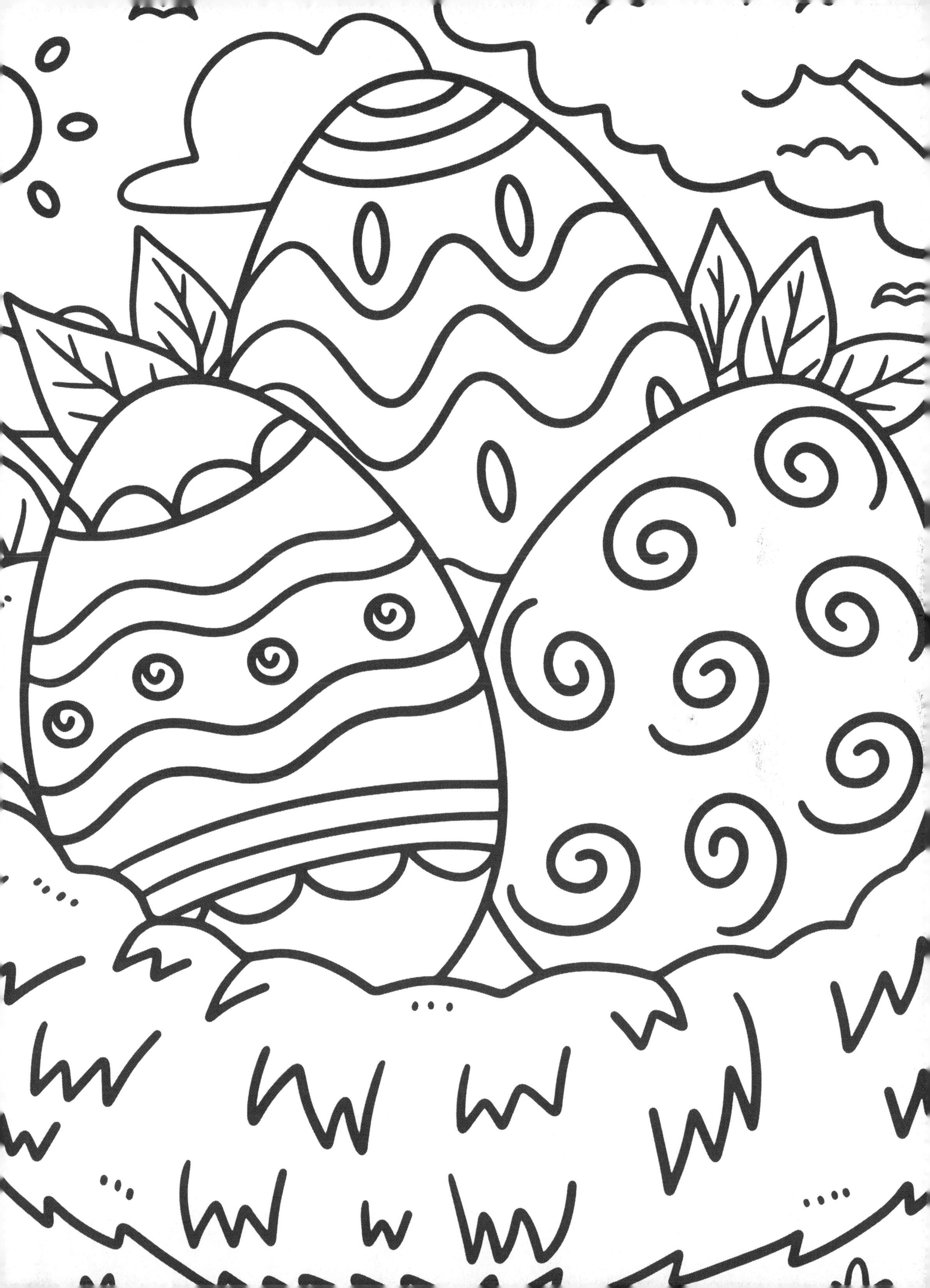

EASTER COLORING

COLOR & CREATE THE MOST AMAZING EASTER EGGS

THANK YOU
FOR HOPPING ALONG!

YOU'VE REACHED THE END OF OUR EASTER ADVENTURE. WE HOPE YOU HAD A WONDERFUL TIME COLORING, PLAYING, AND LEARNING. KEEP EXPLORING, KEEP CREATING, AND REMEMBER—EVERY DAY CAN BE FILLED WITH A LITTLE BIT OF EASTER MAGIC!

HAPPY EASTER AND SEE YOU NEXT TIME!

Made in United States
Orlando, FL
03 March 2025

Daily Book Scanning Log

Name: _____ Date: _____ # of Scanners: _____

BIN #	BOOKS COMPLETED	# OF PAGES	NOTES / EXCEPTIONS
Bin 1			
Bin 2			
Bin 3			
Bin 4			
Bin 5			
Bin 6			
Bin 7			
Bin 8			
Bin 9			
Bin 10			
Bin 11			
Bin 12			
Bin 13			
Bin 14			
Bin 15			
Bin 16			
Bin 17			
Bin 18			
Bin 19			
Bin 20			
Bin 21			
Bin 22			
Bin 23			
Bin 24			
Bin 25			
Bin 26			
Bin 27			
Bin 28			
Bin 29			
Bin 30			
Bin 31			
Bin 32			
Bin 33			
Bin 34			
Bin 35			
Bin 36			
Bin 37			
Bin 38			
Bin 39			
Bin 40			

(BOOKS / LIBROS) TOTAL: _____ / 600

(PAGES / PAGINAS) TOTAL: _____

SHIFT: _____ STATION #: _____